W9-AUX-137
WITHDRAWN
BELMONT PUBLIC LIBRARY

ANIMAL MYSTERIES

A CHAPTER BOOK

Sonia Black

children's press®

A Division of Scholastic Inc.

New York Toronto London Auckland Sydney

Mexico City New Delhi Hong Kong

Danbury, Connecticut

J
590
BLA
22.50

To my aunt, Carmen, with love

ACKNOWLEDGMENTS

The author and publisher would like to thank all those who gave their time and knowledge to help with this book. In particular, special thanks go to Dr. Kenneth J. Lohmann, Department of Biology, University of North Carolina at Chapel Hill and Dr. Nicola S. Clayton, Director of Studies in Natural Sciences, Clare College, University of Cambridge.

Library of Congress Cataloging-in-Publication Data

Black, Sonia.
Animal mysteries : a chapter book / by Sonia Black.— 1st ed.
p. cm. — (True tales)
Includes bibliographical references and index.
ISBN 0-516-25187-2 (lib. bdg.) 0-516-25456-1 (pbk.)
1. Animals—Miscellanea—Juvenile literature. I. Title. II. Series.
QL49.B625 2005
590—dc22

2004028455

© 2005 Nancy Hall, Inc.
Published in 2005 by Children's Press, an imprint of Scholastic Library Publishing.
All rights reserved. Published simultaneously in Canada.
Printed in the United States of America.

CHILDREN'S PRESS and associated logos are trademarks and or registered trademarks of Scholastic Library Publishing. SCHOLASTIC and associated logos are trademarks and or registered trademarks of Scholastic Inc.

1 2 3 4 5 6 7 8 9 10 R 14 13 12 11 10 09 08 07 06 05

CONTENTS

INTRODUCTION

Meet four fascinating animals. They are loggerhead sea turtles, alligators, scrub jays, and apes called "lion killers." You will learn incredible things about these animals.

For example, newborn loggerhead sea turtles swim to regions far away from their hatching places. After many years at sea, female loggerheads find their way back home again to nest. How do they do that?

Alligators have hundreds of bumps all over their jaws. These bumps help the alligators to hunt. How do the bumps work?

Scrub jays do things that show they remember what happened in the past. How is this possible?

The animals called lion killers look like chimpanzees. However, they look like gorillas, too. Some researchers say they are neither of these animals. What are they?

Scientists have been studying these animal mysteries for a long time. Let's find out the answers they have discovered.

CHAPTER ONE

SEA TURTLES ON THE MOVE

It is a hot summer night. Kenneth and Catherine Lohmann are at a beach in Boca Raton, Florida. They are here with a team of workers. They are watching and waiting for turtle eggs to hatch.

Kenneth and Catherine are marine biologists. The husband and wife team is studying loggerhead sea turtles.

Catherine Lohmann

A loggerhead sea turtle on a Florida beach

During the summer months, a female loggerhead comes ashore to lay a **clutch** of eggs about every two weeks. Each clutch may contain about 100 to 130 eggs.

The turtles bury the soft, leathery eggs in the sand and return to the water. After about sixty days, the eggs are ready to hatch. The Lohmanns and their team don't have

A sea turtle laying her eggs in the sand

Newly hatched sea turtles

long to wait. Soon, a great swarm of **hatchlings** wriggle out from their sandy nests. The hatchlings scramble over the sandy shore. They follow the moonlight reflecting off the ocean. They head straight into the water and swim into the waves. The waves take them farther and farther out to sea.

The Lohmanns and their team gently scoop up

A hatchling

Baby sea turtles are less than 2 inches (5 centimeters) long when first hatched.

many hatchlings before they get to the water. They put the baby turtles in a big cooler. Off they go to the team's laboratory. There, the team begins experiments to study the mystery of loggerhead turtles.

What is the mystery? When the hatchlings make it out to sea, they begin a very long journey. They will migrate, or travel, about 9,000 miles (14,484 kilometers) around the Atlantic Ocean. They will travel along a warm **current** of water called the North Atlantic Gyre. The Gyre runs all the way to the coasts of Spain and Africa. If the turtles should go outside of the Gyre, they could end up in very cold water and die.

The turtles spend many years at sea. They are gone for sometimes five, ten, fifteen years or more. After these many years away, female loggerheads return to the nesting ground where they were born.

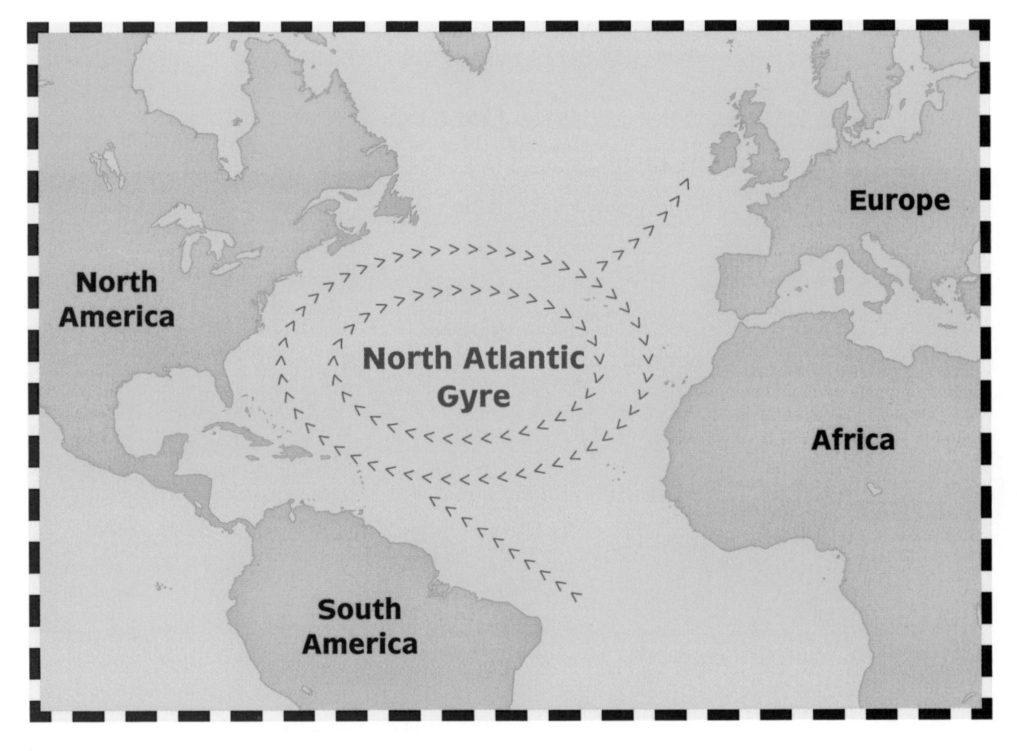

North Atlantic Gyre

Many people have wondered how the turtles find their way back. What helps them to **navigate** and not get lost? The Lohmanns believed that the answer had something to do with the ocean's **magnetic fields**.

The ocean has many magnetic fields. The North Atlantic Gyre flows along one of these. The Lohmanns believed that the turtles have a special sense that leads them to the Gyre's magnetic field. They call this the turtles' "magnetic map." The Lohmanns and their team conducted experiments with the turtles to test this **theory.**

Loggerhead sea turtles spend many years at sea.

A hatchling wearing a swimsuit

First, they filled a round swimming tank with sea water and put it in a dark room. They kept it dark so the turtles could not see where they were going. Then, they tested the turtles one at a time.

The team put a tiny blue swimsuit on each young turtle and placed the turtle in the tank. The swimsuit had wires attached. The wires were connected to a computer in another room. The computer recorded all of the turtle's movements.

The tank was hooked up with wires, too. These wires made the water imitate different magnetic fields of the ocean. The turtles always swam toward the one that matched that of the North Atlantic Gyre.

In the end, the Lohmanns proved that their theory was correct. These turtles had never been in water. Still, they could sense the differences in the magnetic fields. Their magnetic map acts like a compass. It points them in the right direction on their long migration. It guides them to the magnetic field of the warm North Atlantic Gyre.

No one knows as yet just how the loggerhead turtle's magnetic map actually works. And no one knows exactly why it swims so far away. Scientists do know, though, that the loggerhead turtle might soon become **endangered**.

The Lohmanns' studies will work to **conserve** these animals. Kenneth explains, "To help an animal, it is important to know as much about it as possible. This includes knowing what food it eats, what **predators** it must avoid, and how the animal finds its way through its **habitat**."

Kenneth and Catherine Lohmann are working to save loggerhead sea turtles.

CHAPTER TWO

AN ALLIGATOR'S BUMPS

The Rockefeller Wildlife **Refuge** in Louisiana is on thousands of acres of **marshland**. All kinds of animals are found there, including birds, fish, turtles, and alligators. The refuge protects the animals, some of which are endangered **species** (SPEE-sheez).

Many scientists visit the refuge to study the animals. Daphne Soares is one of them.

Daphne Soares

A marsh is home to many animals, including these alligators.

What is the purpose of the bumps on an alligator's face?

Daphne visited the refuge in 1999. She planned to study the brains of birds and reptiles. One day, however, she was riding in a truck with a large alligator. Daphne noticed hundreds of little bluish-colored bumps all over the alligator's face. There were bumps on its mouth, its jaws, and around its eyes and nose. When she asked other scientists what the bumps were for, no one knew.

Daphne decided to find out. She studied everything about alligators. She learned how alligators hunt.

The alligator hunts mostly at night. It

lies very still in the water, close to the surface. Its body is almost hidden underwater. Only the top of its head and its long upper jaw can be seen. Sometimes its eyes are closed.

Suddenly, without any warning, the alligator pounces. It opens its large jaws and snatches its **prey** (PRAY). This could be a crab, frog, fish, snake, or some other small animal. In one big gulp, the alligator swallows it.

When an alligator hunts, only the top of its head can be seen.

An alligator sneaks up on its prey.

Daphne was puzzled. How does the alligator know the small animal is there? She thought about how the alligator lies in the water. She noticed that its bumpy jaws rest right at the surface. That is where the air and water meet. She wondered if the bumps help alligators to hunt by letting them know when prey is nearby.

Daphne went to the Marine Biological Laboratory in Massachusetts to test her idea.

They had special equipment for her experiments. They also had twenty alligators. Daphne set to work.

She kept the laboratory dark. It looked like nighttime, when alligators hunt. A camera that takes pictures in the dark was set up. There were also machines to record the alligators' actions. Daphne did the same experiments with different alligators. Each one reacted the same way.

Daphne holding an alligator

In one experiment, Daphne placed an alligator in a tank of fresh water. Very quietly, she dropped one tiny droplet of water in the tank. The droplet made ripples in the water. When the alligator's head was completely underneath the water, the

Water droplet

alligator did not notice the ripples. When its head was all the way out of the water, it did not notice the ripples. But when its jaws were lying right along the water's surface, the alligator acted differently. It sprang in the direction of the ripples.

Next Daphne covered the alligator's ears with plastic. Now it could not hear. She

An alligator's bumps are sensory organs that let it know when prey is near

added the water droplet. Still, it sprang towards the spot where the droplet hit the water.

Then Daphne covered up the alligator's bumpy snout. Again, she put in the droplet. This time, the alligator did not react.

Daphne realized that these bumps were **sensory organs**. They made the alligator's skin very sensitive to touch. When something hit the water, the water pressure in that spot changed. The bumps made the alligator feel that change. This is how the alligator could sense even the smallest movement in the water.

Daphne called the bumps "pressure receptors." Now she wanted to know how these pressure receptor bumps actually worked. Daphne looked inside an alligator's skull. The bumps were attached to **nerves**.

The nerves were connected to one big nerve. This nerve **stimulates** the skin and muscles of the alligator's face. It is attached to the brain. The alligator's brain controls all of the animal's actions.

Daphne had figured it out. When the water pressure changes, the bumps vibrate. Then a chain reaction happens. The nerves from the bumps warn the big nerve. This big nerve sends the message to the alligator's brain. The brain gets the message and makes the alligator snap up its prey.

Some scientists believe the bumps may help the alligators do other things, too. What could those things be? More research is being done to find out.

Scientists continue to study the alligator's mysterious bumps.

CHAPTER THREE

THE SCRUB JAY'S AMAZING MEMORY

Our memory is what lets us remember things from our past. Scientists call this **episodic memory**. For example, you can probably remember what you did for your birthday. You know that event happened in the past.

For years, scientists believed only people had episodic memory. Doctor Nicky Clayton believes animals can remember in this way, too. Her research is helping to change the way other scientists think.

Nicky Clayton

People are able to remember events that happened in the past. Can animals?

Nicky is a professor at the University of Cambridge in England. She does research on animals and memory. For nine years, Nicky has studied Western scrub jays. She discovered that scrub jays can remember events from their past, just like people do. They use their memories to decide what to do in the present. They can even use their memories to plan for the future.

Nicky became interested in studying the birds when she was teaching at the University of California. She saw lots of Western scrub jays there. Students and teachers often ate lunch outdoors.

Scrub jay

When they finished eating, there was food left on the ground. Scrub jays hungrily gathered up bits of leftovers.

Nicky was fascinated watching these birds. "Scrub jays are famous for **caching** (KASH-ing)," she said. "They hide or bury their leftovers for later. They depend on their memory to go back and get it."

Scrub jays hide all kinds of foods, including olives, beetles, earthworms, and fruits. Some of these foods go bad. The birds need to know when to go back and get the food before this happens.

Some foods rot more quickly than others. Did the birds know this? Could the birds remember how long ago they hid their food? Would this allow them to go back and find the food before it rotted?

Nicky filled ice cube trays with sand.

Nicky wanted to find the answer. She worked with Tony Dickinson, who is also a professor at the University of Cambridge. Together they tested how good the jays were at remembering their caches.

In her laboratory, she prepared ice-cube trays filled with sand. These were for the birds to hide their caches in.

In one experiment, Nicky gave the birds worms and peanuts to bury in the trays. Jays prefer fresh worms to peanuts. They do not eat worms once they have gone bad. Sometimes, Nicky let the birds recover the hidden items a few hours later, when the worms were still fresh. At other times, five days went by before she let the birds go back to find the worms. By then the worms had rotted.

The birds were allowed to cache and recover the worms and peanuts from different trays on different days. This was done to make sure that they had to remember which foods they cached and where. They also had to keep track of time in order to know whether it was worth it to recover the worms.

Nicky found that the birds quickly learned not to search for worms if they had cached them five days earlier. However, if the worms had been cached just a few hours earlier, the birds did recover the still-fresh worms. Later experiments showed they could learn that different **perishable** foods had different **decay rates**. The birds had no problem keeping track of how long ago they cached different perishable foods.

Birds without any experience that foods can go bad continued to search for worms. This shows that the birds are not born knowing how long it takes for items to decay. They need to learn from experience.

Some scientists do not agree with Nicky's findings. They believe one can train animals

A scrub jay eating a worm from the tray.

to behave in certain ways or that animals just act out of habit. They do not think that animals act from memory.

Other scientists agree with Nicky's conclusion that scrub jays do not act by chance. Nicky says that, without a doubt, "They have a sense of the passage of time."

Is this scrub jay remembering where its cache is?

CHAPTER FOUR

MYSTERY APES

The Bili forest is in the Democratic Republic of Congo in Africa. A strange type of animal lives in the Bili forest. Some people say it has a body like a gorilla and a face like a chimpanzee. It is not a gorilla, though. And it is not a chimpanzee. What is it?

No one seems to know for sure. Researchers are trying to find the answer.

Karl Ammann is with one of the research groups. He is a wildlife photographer.

Karl Ammann

The mystery ape lives in the Bili forest in the Democratic Republic of Congo.

On a trip to the Congo, he found a skull of one of the mystery animals. He wanted to know more about them. Karl hired native hunters to track down the strange apes in the thick forest. He became one of the first people to get pictures of them. In the pictures, the apes looked like very big chimpanzees.

Shelly Williams is a **primatologist**. She is also studying the strange animals. She has taken trips to the Congo to look for them, too. She made friends with village people who live there. The villagers had seen the mystery animals many times. They named the animals "lion killers" because they are such huge creatures. The villagers guided Shelly into the forest.

Two skulls of the mystery apes

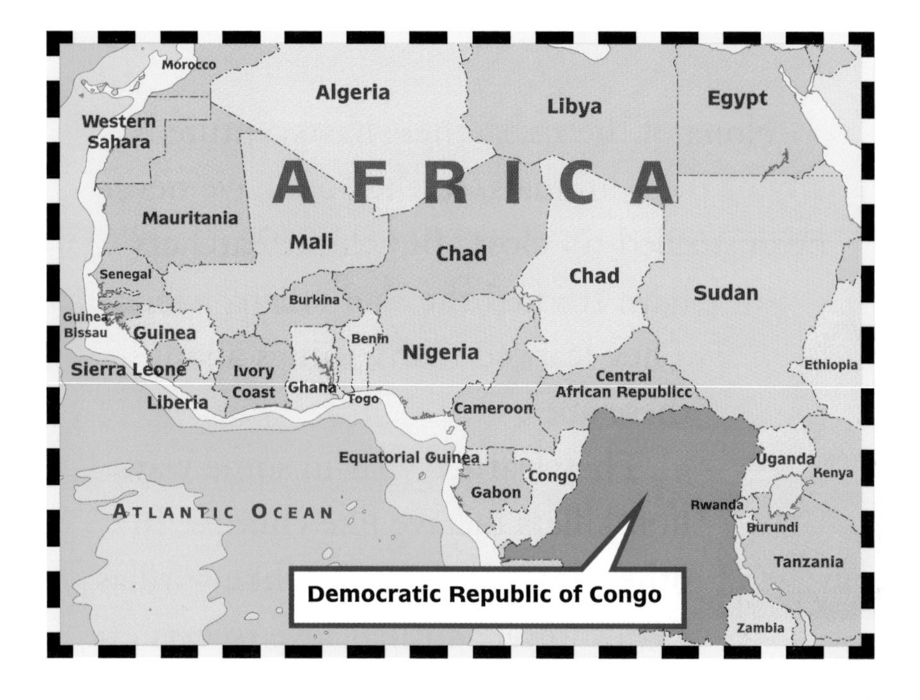

They came upon a family of lion killers. Shelly quickly videotaped the fast-moving animals.

On film, some look to be more than 6 feet (2 meters) tall. They have large hands and feet. Their faces are flatter than those of gorillas.

Shelly Williams holding a cast of a lion killer's footprint

None of the researchers have captured any of these animals, so the apes have never been studied up close. But the researchers have studied the lion killers' habitat. They learned many things about these apes.

Gorilla

They learned that in some ways, lion killers behave like chimps. In other ways, they behave like gorillas. For example, gorillas love to eat meat and fish. Chimpanzees eat a lot of fruit. Lion killers eat mostly fruit, too.

Chimpanzees like to sleep high up in trees. This helps keep them safe from hyenas, lions, and leopards. These animals attack and eat chimpanzees.

A chimpanzee with her young, high in a tree

A lion killer's nest

Lion killers, however, are not afraid of any of these animals. They don't like to climb trees like chimpanzees. They sleep on the ground like gorillas do. They pile up roots, sticks, grass, and leaves and make a big nest in which to sleep. They make these nests near swampy riverbeds.

The researchers collected things they found in the lion killers' nests. They collected samples of hair and the animals' droppings. They even found lion killers' footprints. The footprints had dried in mud and formed natural molds. They gathered up the footprint molds.

Measuring a lion killer's footprint

Scientists at several laboratories conducted studies on the ape samples. The footprint molds showed that these animals' feet are bigger than those of gorillas.

Ed Louis works at the Henry Doorly Zoo in Omaha, Nebraska. He studies **DNA**. DNA is found in all living things. The ape droppings and hair contain the animals' DNA. Ed compared the DNA in the mystery apes' droppings with the DNA in droppings from gorillas, **bonobos**, and chimpanzees. So far, his tests show that lion killers have more characteristics of chimpanzees than of gorillas or bonobos.

So what really are these mystery animals? Are they gorillas? Are they chimpanzees? Are they the offspring from gorillas mating with chimpanzees? Or are they a brand-new species of ape altogether?

Experts in Karl Ammann's group believe the animals are giant chimpanzees that act like gorillas. Shelly Williams' group believes they are most likely a new breed of giant apes. Until more research is done, the lion killers of the Bili forest remain a mystery.

Scientists continue to do research on the lion killers of the Bili forest.

GLOSSARY

bonobo a small kind of chimpanzee

cache (KASH) to hide or store food; a hidden place where food is stored

clutch a group of eggs laid by a female animal

conserve to keep something from being wasted or used up

current the movement of water in a river or ocean

decay rate the time it takes for food to spoil

DNA a long chain of information that fits inside the cells of all living things

endangered in danger of dying out or becoming extinct

episodic memory a working of the brain that lets us remember past experiences

habitat the surroundings where an animal or a plant naturally lives

hatchling a baby animal that has just come out of its shell

magnetic field the area around a magnet where the magnet's pull is felt

marshland an area of wet, grassy land

navigate to steer or find one's way

nerves fibers that carry messages between the brain and other parts of the body

perishable likely to spoil

predator an animal that kills other animals for food

prey (PRAY) an animal that is hunted by another animal for food

primatologist a scientist who studies primates, a group of animals that includes monkeys, apes, and humans

refuge a place that provides protection or shelter

sensory organ a body part that gives the brain information about the world

species (SPEE-sheez) a single kind of living thing

stimulate to cause something to happen

theory an idea that tries to explain something

FIND OUT MORE

Sea Turtles on the Move
http://www.ncaquariums.com/turtletrails
Track loggerhead sea turtles as they migrate.

An Alligator's Bumps
http://www.eparks.org/marine_and_coastal /marine_wildlife/alligator.asp
Find out more about alligators and their hunting habits.

The Scrub Jay's Amazing Memory
http://www.exploratorium.edu/memory
How good is *your* memory? Play the memory games on this site and discover how your brain remembers.

Mystery Apes
http://media.animal.discovery.com/fansites/janegoodall /interactives/greatape/greatape.html
Learn more about our closest living relatives, the great apes.

More Books to Read

Crocodiles and Alligators by Seymour Simon, HarperCollins, 2001

Great Apes by Barbara Taylor, Anness Publishing, 2003

Jays by Mary Ann McDonald, Child's World, 1999

They Swim the Seas: The Mystery of Animal Migration by Seymour Simon, Harcourt, 1998

INDEX

PHOTO CREDITS

Cover, 15, 19 (bottom)**, 40** © Digital Vision
1, 4 (top left)**, 6, 7, 9, 10, 13** © Kenneth J. Lohmann
3, 12 © Corel
4 (top right)**, 25** © Fotosearch/Creatas
4 (bottom left) © Bill Terry /Photo Network/PictureQuest
4 (bottom right)**, 36, 37, 38, 41, 43** © Karl Ammann
8 © Kelvin Aitken/Peter Arnold, Inc.
16 © Gal Haspel
17, 19 (top left)**, 19** (top right)**, 22, 23, 29** (right)**, 30, 32** © AbleStock
18 © Adam Britton
20 © Phil Coale/AP Wide World
21 © Daphne Soares
26, 29 (left)**, 31, 33** © Ian Cannell & Nicky Clayton/University of Cambridge
27 © Comstock/Getty Images
28 © Bill Terry/Photo Network /PictureQuest
35 © Sharon Bailey/Stock Connection/PictureQuest
39 © Nati Harnik/AP Wide World

MEET THE AUTHOR

For many years, Sonia Black has worked in children's publishing as an editor and author. She loves writing for children. Among her books for young readers are *Hanging Out with Mom, Mommy's Bed, Jumping the Broom, Home for the Holidays, Mae Jemison,* and *Plenty of Penguins*. She enjoys taking trips to her beloved homeland, Jamaica, West Indies. Ms. Black lives in New Jersey with her two precious daughters, Greyson and Evanne, and their pet hamster, Stinky.